drifting through time,
aware of everything
you are.

Dear George,

May I call you dear George? I read your poems 'My gift to you' and felt yourself vividly. I believe your world and you as you are. I love your being as I love my being. I know that you were born to live and go on your way and I was born to live and go on my way. If we could meet each other somewhere it would be wonderful even if the encounter is a moment.

I wrote you because I wanted to communicate you my feeling of encounter with you and I am very happy if you would share your another poems with me. I am scaring if my poor English can not communicate my feeling well.

with love,

Miss Hiromi Sotani
18-9-1 Seta, Setagaya-ku
Tokyo, Japan

VISIONS of YOU

George Betts

Photography: Bob Scales
Illustrations: Thomas A. Woodruff
Celestial Arts Publishing
Millbrae, California 94030

First Printing, December 1971
Second Printing, April 1972
Third Printing, August 1972
Fourth Printing, October 1972
Fifth Printing, June 1973
Sixth Printing, September 1973
Seventh Printing, May 1974
Library of Congress Card No. 76-183409
ISBN 0-912310-07-3
Made in the United States of America

For Donni

The dawn of my life,

like the dawn of today,

is only a memory of my mind,

so important because it

gave me the opportunity to grow,

to become,

what I am

and what I will be,

and I thank you for this day and for my life.

I can't promise you a rose garden.
Promises should be kept once they are made.
I can't make one for the future
 because the future is unknown
and so am I. . . . . .tomorrow.
But don't worry about roses and tomorrow,
  share my warmth with me today.
You can have rainbows and butterflies
  because today is here
   and so are we.
Life must be lived today, you know.
If you worry about tomorrow
  and don't live today,
suddenly you will realize that all you have
  are empty yesterdays.

I want my freedom
　　but I also want you.

　　Can I have both?

　　Are you different?

Will you give me new freedom to enjoy
Those things I would miss if you were gone?

I'm drifting - - as an endless wave

Close, then far away

                    only to return
                Close, then far away.
    What would a wave be
                without movement?
    What would I be without change?

In you I see
the strength of mankind,
the beauty of nature,
and the love of God.

It was hard to say goodbye to a
million dreams,
a thousand promises,
and you.
Like reading a good book,
I was reluctant to finish the last page,
But the memories of you are written
well within my life.
They are the things that can't be taken from me.
I have set aside a book for them
on my private shelf,
An adventure in the volumes of love.

Many people
come and go
through
the doors
of my life,
taking what
they need
and
giving what
they can.
Our moments
were only
seconds
of a
lifetime
but so
important
because we
shared
what we
could.
Only a
glimpse
of the
sun
but
enough
to warm
the
heart.

The question is not

"Have I taken more than I have given?"

but

"Have I taken something

you   really   didn't   want

to   give?"

How can we be lovers
   if we aren't even friends?
Relationships develop so fast.
      Push — — no time for tomorrow.
Accomplish everything today
            but wait,

please slow down,
 let me show you
  what I am,
   where I am,   *and*
  where I am going.

Look around,
reach out,

there's a human being
to be discovered.

i stand in darkness . . .

wondering

if

light will ever come my way again

The times we shared together
are remembered now only in my mind.
A small but important part,
shaping today's world
with yesterday's memories.
Another chapter in the
unwritten biography of my life,
never to be experienced again,
remembered only in my mind.

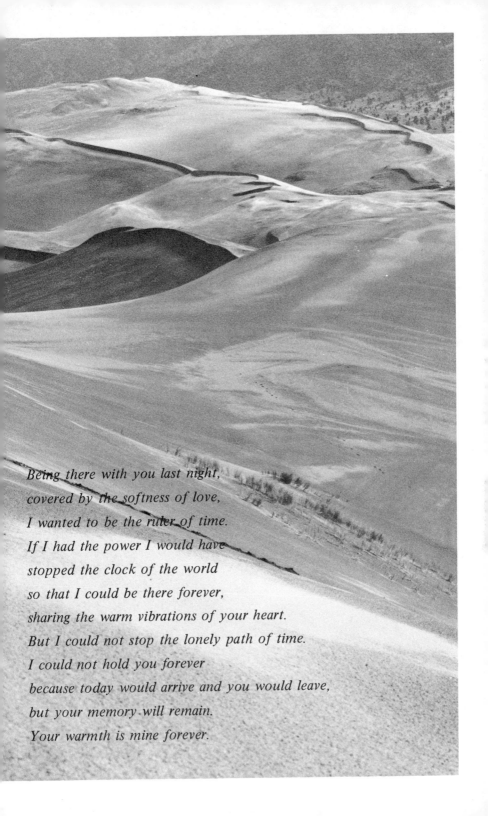

Being there with you last night,
covered by the softness of love,
I wanted to be the ruler of time.
If I had the power I would have
stopped the clock of the world
so that I could be there forever,
sharing the warm vibrations of your heart.
But I could not stop the lonely path of time.
I could not hold you forever
because today would arrive and you would leave,
but your memory will remain.
Your warmth is mine forever.

He was so happy
      running along the beach
            building sand castles - -
I watched him laugh and smile,
      so innocent,
            and so young,
but, suddenly I was saddened
      because of tomorrow - -
            He must grow up.
His sand castles will wash away
and be replaced with adulthood
      and responsibility.
It's too bad he'll have to learn
      about prejudice, hatred,
            and war.

You come to see me
only when you're down.
Walk in,
unload your problems,
and then
"I feel better, Thank you!"
Why don't you come over
when you're up?
I'd love to see you laugh and smile
and tell me how beautiful
life can be.
Can't you tell I'm caught
inside today?
Sorry, I can't listen,
but look at me.
Can't you tell . . . . .   Sometimes I need you
not to talk,
but to listen,

Please notice me.

I've offered you a part of me,
      something I don't give
            too many people.
I thought you understood,
      but I guess I was wrong.
You seemed to run.
Games were the thing for you,
      but I won't play.
I've been down that road before.

Yesterday . . . Seven Years Ago

> *Riding down the highway, seventy miles an hour*
> *I concentrate on the white lines,*
> > *not connected,*
> *but following one after another.*
> *Life is like that,*
> > *one day after another, time moves on*

so I must move on down the road
trying to put the lines together
so I can understand the traveled miles of my life.
Maybe then I will be able to enjoy
    the many untraveled miles that are before me,
but first I must connect the white lines.

The day Tommy Brown left
was like any other cloudy day,
covered with a silent softness,
sprinkled with rain,

and a rare glimpse of sun.

I wanted to tell you about Tommy Brown,

but you didn't know him.

>   *You wouldn't understand.*

That's funny!

Maybe I don't understand.

Why do I feel so empty?

>   *He'll be back.*

Two years in the Army isn't forever,

>   *but he didn't want to go.*

He was forced

>   *because he's a citizen*

and he must serve.

>   *Good luck, Tommy Brown.*

My first memories of you
show reflections of a
shy and anxious look.
You were ready to grow
but did not know the way.
"Be my friend" were the
words that started our
journey.
Many people have traveled
with me since I met you.
Some stay minutes while
others linger through
passing seasons.
Somehow you're different
from the rest.
Many miles are behind us
now.
We have both changed.
Our growth cannot be
measured;
neither can our love.

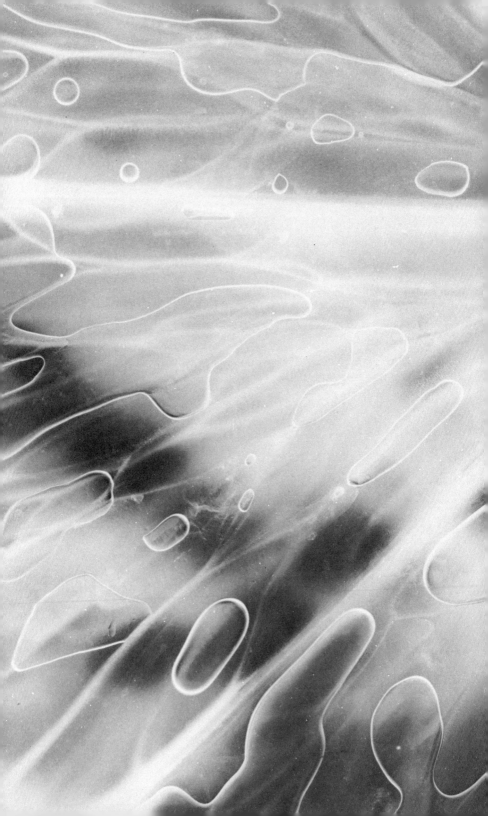

Help! I don't understand my mind.
It's moving too fast.
            I'm being left behind.
Wait! Don't leave me!
I know you have so many things to do.
                        but wait . . .

Let me get it together.
I've got to understand the past
                    so I can bury it.
Wait! Give me time . . .
            then we can move on together.

Today will be a pleasant memory . . .
tomorrow
because we cared enough to give
the only thing we have, ourselves.

I look inside
and find that
life has been
good to me,
giving me the
ability to see
where I have been
and where I am going . . .

To find the one I searched for,
To find the love I've wanted,
To live the life I now have
has made me a contented man.

There seems to be a gentle feeling of peace within my soul for you today.
I saw the ocean, and for a brief moment, I understood.

I was conceived in a world
beyond my grasp, beyond my
knowledge. A world for me to be
born in . . . . and to die.
But what about the "in-between" time?
Can I connect birth, life, and death
into a flowing stream of consciousness?
The only decision that is truly mine
is how I choose to spend my days, hours,
and minutes.

Will I develop my "being" into something
of significance? Will I find contentment
and enjoyment deep within the walls of my
being, or will I wander through life blindly,
unaware of my own purpose? Will I find this
for myself or will I perish? Only I can decide!

I wonder if you realize

how much I care for you?
I want to make this your day,
a tribute to you.
    A time to share . . .
       a gentle smile,
          a soft caress,
             and a tenderness
               of two hearts
    touching
           on this your day.

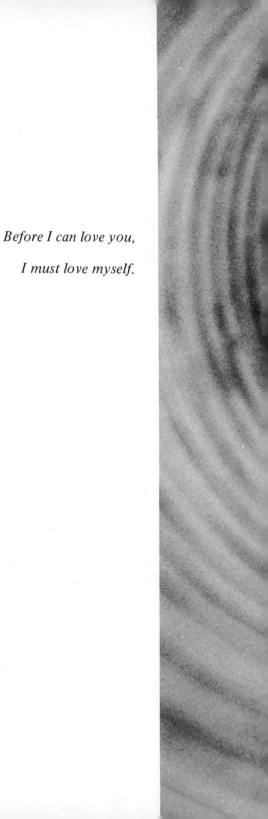

Before I can love you,

I must love myself.

The in-between time

after love has gone

is filled with wonderment,

waiting for the heart

to cry out again in joy

because someone smiles

and says hi.

It's as if we never loved each other.
We both seem so different now,
pulled apart,

        separated,

             and alone.
Even your smile seems different.
Am I important to you

    or am I just another person
lost forever,

      only a memory of your mind?

I have no fear of rejection by you
for I am the only one who can truly

reject me.

A flower blossoms
with water
and sunshine,

A woman,
with warmth
and love.

The tide rushes in and
covers my footprints,
leaving the sand fresh
for another adventure.

My life is like the sand.
People journey through my
mind and leave their footprints,
but then the tide rushes in.

Today I'm here with you and
I'm very happy. I have found
a friend, someone to share
my garden, my dreams, and my being.
It's very misty as I sit here
watching you walk along the beach,
aware of the depth of everything
around you.

Now you are out of my sight but
I'm still close. I feel your
warmth. The waves are moving
closer to me now.
I'm being engulfed with life.
All of its beauty and
*   magnitude are ours.*

It's been a long time, but I still remember.

You say you love me,

    that you accept me,

But why do you frown when I act differently?

Can't you accept the different sides of me?

I must change as I live.

Don't ask me to sacrifice my growth

    to meet your expectations.

        I am what I am.

If you do love me, you'll understand.

A friend of mine died across the street
about a year ago,
a prisoner in a rest home,
made to meet his needs
as best it could.
I watched him grow old
as I grew up.
He lived alone in his home of memories
and bright flowers in the summer.
We smiled
and shared
many trips to the grocery store,
but I really didn't know him.
I was too young.
Now I sit in an apartment
while the snow falls
gently to the ground as it did
about a year ago when he died
across the street.

Whenever I think of you,
I find myself
drifting through time,
aware of everything
you are.

Miles separate us,

    Memories bind us.

We are apart,

    But we are together.

You love me today.

What more could I want?

*The greatest gift
you can give me is
the opportunity for me
to be me and for me to
let you be you.*

When I look into a mirror,
I see a man striving to be.

How lonely it must be
searching for happiness,
unaware of the beauty you possess,
never realizing how much warmth
you really give.

If I could,
    I would show you
        how you are
            through my eyes.
Then you could see
how important you are.
My world is happy
        because of you.

I have invested my future in today.

I thought of you when
I returned to the beach.
The sound of the crashing waves
reminded me of the night with you.

I heard the waves that night,
but they were just the props
for our performance.
We were both beautiful,
saying our lines with our hearts,
receiving applause only from our souls.

Now that I have returned,
I wonder why the curtain had to close,
leaving me
on an empty stage.

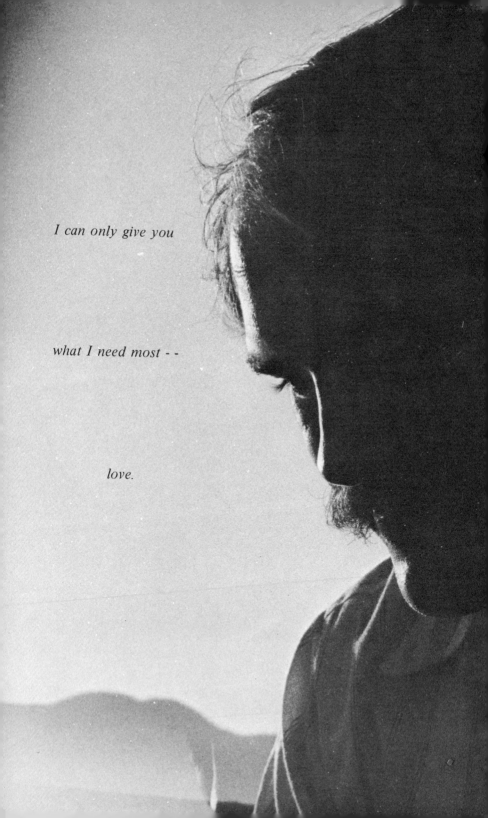

I can only give you

what I need most - -

love.

I can only give you

what I need most - -

love.

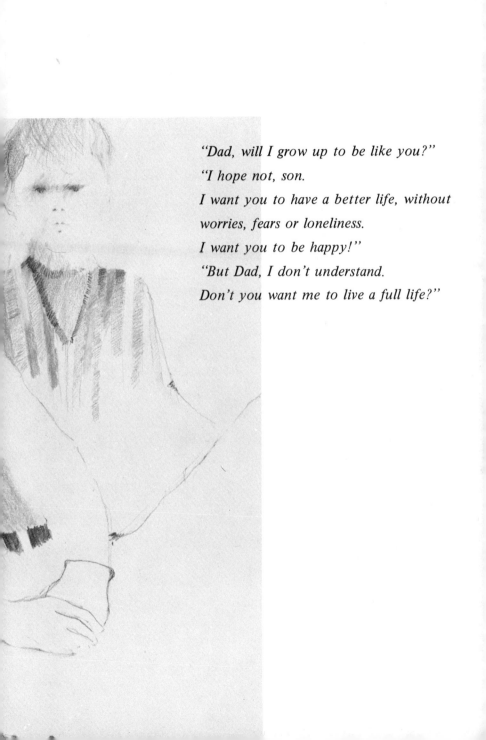

"Dad, will I grow up to be like you?"
"I hope not, son.
I want you to have a better life, without worries, fears or loneliness.
I want you to be happy!"
"But Dad, I don't understand.
Don't you want me to live a full life?"

I have a commitment to you,
a commitment
written in the wind,
giving you my love
as I live.

Our friendship will not be erased by the passage of time.

Cowboy hats and plastic guns
were my style as I moved west
until they were left behind
in a large box full of toys.

Marbles, yo-yo's, and bicycles
continued with me. I still
remember them, but somewhere
they were lost.

Long hair, wide ties, and
bell-bottoms helped me find you
but now they are changing. Will
you still be here when my hair
is short and nicely trimmed?

*I cannot predict
what I will be.
I can only live
what I am.*

To love you totally,

I must be able to

accept all sides of you.

The last frontier of man

will be to understand himself.

When I hold back
because of a fear
of rejection by you,
I find I reject myself.

When I reach out

and find you,

I also find me.

We all have dreams.
Some come true
While others become plays
Never to be performed.

The train of love is traveling
along the tracks of time.
I know you are waiting
                    at a distant station,

a traveler in your own right,
riding the rails that carry
> *you away from the past,*
always in hope of finding
> *someone to share your journey.*

I'll share my candle with you,

it's warm and alive

At times I must leave you
and go deep inside
where I can explore
the mysteries of my mind,
*   of my being.*

I must settle things
*   with myself . . .*

then,
*   I am able to travel*
back to you
and we can continue together
but at times,
*   I must leave you.*

Watching you walk out the door
and down the street
reminded me of myself
when I was young.

I can still remember my mom
standing in the doorway
the first day of school.
She wanted me to go,
because she knew I had to,
but at the same time
she wanted me to stay
because she knew I would
never return the same.

Now I stand and watch you,
Nomastay, my beautiful friend.

We have met,
strangers among strangers
searching for meaning
through people and experiences

Loneliness had been our companion
like a suitcase of past advertures
carried with us
providing some security.

Our adventure provided warmth,
an added dimension to our lives.
We gave to each other
even though it wasn't expected.

Between passing days
and fleeting romances
our friendship has grown,
never defined by words.

Because of the way you are
I have wanted to give you a gift.
Perfume would have been nice
but its fragrance is always fleeting.

Flowers would have added warmth
for moments, but nothing tangible
can last forever.

Nothing I have to give
would represent my
true feelings for you.

Finally one day, clustered
among the colorful aspens
and the sounds of a rushing brook,
I discovered my gift for you.

All that I can give you is time
time to grow . . .
                    to share . . .
                              to love . . .
                                        as only you can do.

My demands of you are simple.
Blossom, my friend, into the
beautiful flower I see inside.

Share your warmth as you love.
Spread your happiness as you give,
and remember me as I pass
through your mind
like gentle waves on the drifting sand.

Because we are not afraid of tomorrow,
nor restricted by yesterday,
we are able to love today.

I think the most essential tools I have developed in my life are my sensitivity and awareness of myself, others, and nature.

I am presently developing my life at the University of Northern Colorado in Greeley, Colorado, where I am teaching psychology while completing a doctoral degree in Psychology, Counseling, and Guidance. Teaching, for me, is not a job, but a commitment to the growth and development of those with whom I come in contact.

My writing becomes a roadmap, not to show me where I am going, but to let me re-live where I have been. I share it with you in the hope that you can add another piece to this puzzle called life. I feel that by sharing ourselves we can open avenues for others to travel, to share, and to grow.